Best Western and Other Poems

The Gerald Cable Book Award Series

Love Fugue
Shulamith Wechter Caine

Dime Store Erotics
Ann Townsend

Bodies that Hum
Beth Gylys

Inventing Difficulty
Jessica Greenbaum

Why They Grow Wings
Nin Andrews

Odd Botany
Thorpe Moeckel

A Parade of Hands
James Hoch

Lime
Audrey Bohanan

Any Holy City
Mark Conway

Sleeping Upside Down
Kate Lynn Hibbard

What Kills What Kills Us
Kurt S. Olsson

The Odds of Being
Daneen Wardrop

Blue to Fill the Empty Heaven
Joel Friederich

Best Western and Other Poems

Eric Gudas

Silverfish Review Press
Eugene, Oregon

First Edition

Published by

Silverfish Review Press
P.O. Box 3541
Eugene, OR 97403
www.silverfishreviewpress.com

Distributed by

Small Press Distribution
800-869-7553
orders@spdbooks.org
www.spdbooks.org

Library of Congress Cataloging-in-Publication Data

Gudas, Eric.
Best western and other poems / by Eric Gudas. --1st ed.
p. cm.
Includes bibliographical references.
ISBN 978-1-878851-57-4
I. Title.
PS3607.U33B47 2010
811'.6--dc22

2009045983

Manufactured in the United States of America

Contents

Three

Introduction

By Barbara Hamby

We go to poetry for many things: music, beauty, that shiver covering our arms when we read something so beautiful and true that it can't be denied. When I read Shakespeare, I feel as if he is speaking directly to me. His mistress's eyes are nothing like the sun? I'm in his world. And when Keats says, "I have been half in love with easeful death," I'm sitting under that plum tree with him listening to his nightingale. I feel as if I am in the middle of a thought unfolding in the mind of the poet. In the same way I feel as if I am in Yusef Komunyakaa's mind as he looks at the Vietnam War Memorial in Washington. I see the mother brushing her child's hair at the end of the poem just as Komunyakaa does. This is what I look for in poetry—others telling me what it is to be human in their patches in time.

Eric Gudas pulled me into his world as soon as I read the first poem in this book. His is a world of travel, menial jobs, kisses, clotheslines, puking cats, Jehovah's Witness pamphlets, clogged drains, forgotten lovers, a dog's water dish. One of my favorite poems is "945 Pecan Place," which paints a portrait of a marriage filled with the mundane: a wife working at a supermarket, a husband folding clothes, eating toaster waffles, and paying bills—until the last line, in which the husband waits "impatient for your worn-out footsteps at the door." I didn't know it was going to be a love poem until that last line. And I was surprised over and over as I read *Best Western and Other Poems.*

Because this is a book of journeys—to Berlin, along the Pacific Coast Highway, from bachelorhood to marriage. In "For the Annapolis-Baltimore Railway Line," Gudas writes an elegy for travel by rail. "En Route" begins in Rimini and ends in the sky over Kansas City, Missouri, "shining / like stolen jewels spilled at my feet." "Broke in West Berlin" is about that and so much more. In the gorgeous title poem of this collection, a father takes his young son to his mother's funeral. The child has never met his grandmother, who lies in her coffin. He has never seen the relatives, who are mourning this woman, but years later this journey and others like it lead him to other farewells, especially the one that we are always negotiating with our own pasts.

In a letter Keats says, "We hate poetry that has a palpable design on us." Eric Gudas's poems unfold as naturally as one takes a breath, and anyone who writes knows how difficult that is to accomplish. So it is my pleasure to introduce a poet whose design is so woven into the lines of his verse as to seem like watching clouds on a summer afternoon until the clouds begin to take shape and speak to us in a voice so real it might be our own.

For Alyssa and Lily
and in memory of Jane Cooper

A novelist, it is now clear to me, is like those men who wander about in public parks, a huge sack slung over their shoulders, holding in their right hands sticks which have a sharp piece of metal attached to one end. The sharp pointed stick is for impaling any fragments of wastepaper, rags, cigarette butts, any debris that human beings have left lying about under the trees. The capacious sack in which the wanderers stow the litter was handed to them in the early morning and they will have to carry it as long as there is light enough to see what is lying on the grass.

—Caroline Gordon

One

Orange Juice

Four carafes of freshly-squeezed orange juice sit on the conference
room table.
The meeting is over; the governor, thronged by cops and security
agents,
Has left the building—he's riding through the sky in a helicopter.
Now the caterers are cleaning up, breaking down tables, hauling
empty coffee urns
To the waiting vans outside. When I ask a crinkled blue-uniformed
woman, broom in hand,
If it's okay to use the pay phone, she scrunches her mouth
And raises her eyebrows to say, *I don't know.* Maybe she doesn't
speak English.
Maybe she can't tell my face from the governor's face, or from the
faces of the other men
In charcoal suits, who leaned confidentially into the corners
Of the conference room—conferring, their decisions weighty
as weather.

Behind glass the juice is molten yellow, the most real
Color in this huge building, the sky slate gray through venetian
blinds.
Who will drink it? Not the woman sweeping out the hallway, her
eyes intent
On the length of carpet ahead; not the catering guys, their
thick arms
Strained with the weight of the loads they heave upstairs; not the
one cop
Still loitering outside, her bleached-blonde hair slicked back, her belt
heavy with pistol, handcuffs, nightstick.

The juice must be warm by now—warm, but still vivid to the
tongue, tasting of fermented light. Pressed from the fruit's inside,
It flares in the mouth's darkness before entering the bloodstream.
Poured down the drain

It will mix with paint thinner, Coke, rainwater, bleach, urine from
the men pissing
Against buildings all up and down Mission Street, tears even, from
the face of a woman
I saw sobbing into a pay phone on my way to work, her cheeks
stippled with mascara.

Lace Huts

Twenty years ago Jimi Hendrix
played a concert and somebody
made a tape I'm listening to now,
as I sit by my window watching
the trees get tipsy
in the breeze. The crowd
goes wild for one of Jimi's
solos, and don't they get tired
of doing that still, decades
later, with potbellies and bad teeth
and kids in college and mortgages?
But no, they keep on cheering
so I turn off the tape and read
the obituaries: June R. Meeks
was a sixty-nine year-old Methodist
with two sons; Arthur L. Bassford,
fifty-three, excelled at golf,
tennis, and duck-carving. It's all
true, but what about the time
June wrecked her car and the boys
had to drive her everywhere
for two weeks? They used to fight
about it, they had their own lives
and didn't want to bother. . . . Or
when Art carved a duck so perfectly
brown and soft his wife Bonnie
broke down and cried because she wanted
to touch the feathers that weren't there?
The elegiac is mundane,
and so what? The Hendrix
concert's been over for a long time
now, and Jimi's gone back to his hotel
to choke on his vomit and die,
leaving his fans to worse lives—

maybe one of them, sitting right up
in the third row took a bad trip
she hasn't gotten over, and that's her
on the phone now: I'll pick it up
to hear, "I ride a raft
made of my best friend's bones
down the Nile, and all along
the shore are huts made of white lace
and I can hear the screaming
of half-dead infants," or maybe, "Sorry,
sorry, I must have the wrong number."

Best Western

With the dry pop and twang of country music
playing from one speaker in the back of the car,
my father and I drove through North Carolina,
at fifty-five miles per hour,
a purple curtain stretched out over the summer sky.
My father's face was stunned and bitter
as if something beyond his control had bought his memories
for a high price, and he was only now realizing
their loss. We had been driving so long
that our destination seemed almost a secret to us,
to be revealed upon our arrival, and indeed we hesitated
when we got to my grandmother's house
by the ocean, with lazy curtains dawdling by the window
in the breeze. Inside my grandmother's body was laid out,
pale-skinned, her hands crossed. I had never seen her before.
Aunts and uncles, cousins like gnats moved around us, translucent,
as the sun went down. In another room men's voices boomed carelessly,
talking of numbers and shapes, of buildings not yet built.
My father stood by the coffin, grasping its side,
and a blue-haired aunt approached him, rested her hand
on the shoulder of his stiff navy sport coat. "She died
in her sleep," she said. "There was nothing
we could do."

But for my father, I imagine now, his mother had died in
his sleep years before that. She'd died as he slept
at boot camp, she'd died as he reached over and touched
my mother's face on the honeymoon bed. He had run away
at age fourteen, bought a ticket
for some far-away state. . . . Leaving the army,
leaving his wife, never making up his mind,
what need had he for a mother?
And now I think about my mother, and the night he stole me
from her. We drove for hours then, too, sleeping restlessly

in a Holiday Inn somewhere in New England.
I had one pair of underwear and a book; they rested
on the television console as we tossed and turned,
and that was when my mother died for me. She slipped away
in that midnight, and her ghost has kept me running
long after my father grew too old to run with me.

My father found another aunt as we moved toward the door,
toward the car, toward the Best Western motel room registered
in our name. We're very tired, he said, shutting the screen door,
and that was only half a lie, because as soon as we got
into our separate beds we passed into a long, dark sleep.
But if we had taken the exit to the highway,
we could have kept going for days, driving
to distance ourselves from the tendrils of our pasts
that clawed and groped for us
in the suffocating summer dusk.

Kissing in College

I had to go and read
Middlemarch: the book bulged
like a brick in my pocket.
Like Casaubon, I'd spent the day
poring over textbooks, looking
for *the key to all mythologies;*
I was Lydgate, gazing at everyone's
bodies in the cafeteria, in search of
the perfect tissue. I thought
if I hid myself deep in the bowels
of the library, reading *Middlemarch*
all night I would come to understand
my jittery fingers, the burning
behind my eyes—if I finished
Middlemarch my body would fall
from me and I would become wise,
the book smoking like hot gold on the carpet.

Standing outside of the dormitory,
I told you this: "I have to go
read *Middlemarch*." Your lips seemed
about to say the name of that big
book, but instead you pulled me
to you and
                        you kissed me
—your tongue traced the shape
of my lips, your forearms
hugged my ears until I could hear
squirrels bumbling through
the trees, clouds brushing the moon,
the molecules of air around us bouncing
off and off each other. . . .
                                                            How long did we sway
there as students swarmed by

us, their pockets crammed
with notebooks, cigarettes, money,
keys, and matchbooks, our hair
falling in our faces, our mouths widening
to swallow the swirling center
of us. . . . I reached
into your pocket to feel your hip

and your copy of *Middlemarch*
fell to the ground.

Daylight Savings

Today, as we leaned back in the wobbly chairs at our kitchen table, a
radio announcer bleated
That it was eleven when we'd thought it was noon. The morning
seemed suddenly ecstatic: scalding coffee
In my battered tin cup, the *Enterprise* filled with news of another
school board reshuffling, trash cans
Full of egg cartons and plastic strawberry boxes outside the
window. . . . These last months you and I
Have slept long past the alarm's blare each morning, in our
bedroom—dark where ginkgoes
Block the morning light—that we call "the crypt." That time spent
writhing in the green sheets, half-awake
And testy, seems lost, given away. (*My sleeping patterns are corrupt,*
reads the first page of your journal
From last year—the only page that's written on. I have notebooks
like that, too.) On our second night in this house
You picked gardenia blossoms from the bush outside and put them
in a bowl of water on the nightstand;
Of course they turned a sickly russet in a few days and puckered
inward, bound for the trash. Against the alarm clock
Leans a photo of my as-yet-unmarried grandmother sitting by a
wooded lake (how many years before her six children?):
Her clunky, skewed smile, high cheekbones pulling her skin taut in
the 1940s afternoon; but I remember her
In a flimsy green hospital gown, playing round after round of gin
rummy with her best friend Jim, the red-baiting priest, whose
own
Death wasn't far off. As I left for the airport she said, "I'll come to
New York for the weekend when I get out of here,
We can go to dinner at Mama Lucia's." She knew she wasn't getting
any better, but what could I answer?
How many afternoons did I spend in that Bloomington hospital
room, rubbing her back and glancing idly at the TV, going
downstairs

Every couple hours to scrounge cigarette butts from an ashtray
outside the EMERGENCY entrance? Once I bummed one
From a sandbag-bellied security guard at a Tenderloin bus stop, his
face laced with bulging veins, the whites of his eyes a dull pink.
He wheezed handing over the smoke, and cackled, "Tell St. Peter at
the pearly gates, 'I'm sorry, but I just can't wait!'" I'll never forget
him.
Or will I? *Why on earth,* wonders the Italian architect on his
deathbed in my favorite novel, *his memory*
*Should have squandered and destroyed so many days and so many
events, and yet preserved that moment so accurately,*
Bringing it through the years, tempests, and ruins, he did not know.
What will you and I remember
Of our love's (as we say) fullness? Last March, waiting for you to
come down the airplane's accordion-tube
Into the terminal, surrounded by other waiting people—some with
crinkly, heart-shaped balloons, scanning the emerging faces,
Others off to one side reading newspapers—I recalled the Jehovah's
Witnesses pamphlet slipped through
The mail slot one morning: a painting of people all ages and races,
hugging frantically or staggering back to gape
At each other; YOU WILL BE REUNITED WITH YOUR LOVED
ONES IN HEAVEN, it read. How I wish
That other world were real as the half-rotten wooden lawn chairs in
our backyard, where your red sweatpants
Are pinned to the line, and we sit all afternoon reading and eating
almonds, our knees barely touching. . . . Maybe the joy
Of that extra hour is the only afterlife we'll ever have. Omar the
cat—walnut-brown, fat, green-eyed—
Saunters inside, stops, hacks, pukes up grass and pink bile on the
kitchen floor, then pads away,
Proud and disinterested. Tomorrow we will lie in bed past ten, then
eleven, in those book-littered sheets: "Sweetheart,
"We have to get up." "I know." "No, really, we do." "I know, but
listen—just give me fifteen minutes more."

Standing in a Field

It's Sunday night and I'm out for a walk.
The field I'm standing in is soon to become
luxury townhouses, or so I hear. It's weird
standing here, just knowing. I imagine
that if I stand here long enough perhaps
I will become a barely visible part
of a house yet to be built. Maybe
the living room. Perhaps one evening
a couple will be entertaining, and they will look up
and see me, ill-defined, standing before the fireplace.
At first it will scare them—is their house haunted?
Have they had too much to drink? But after they
put their hands through my body, see that I am only an image,
the whole thing will become funny, a novelty.
Maybe later in the evening they will throw darts through me.

I wonder if I flew a kite here, sometime after midnight,
if that kite would become a part of the second floor
of a townhouse. Maybe the master bedroom.
Late at night a man and woman
will be making love. She will be kissing his ear,
her hand on the back of his neck. His hand gripping
her side. They will look up and see
my blue kite, rippling silently above them.
The sweat will dry on their bodies,
and they will stare at the kite for a long time,
until they are convinced it is only a manifestation
of their love. He will dip his mouth to her breast
and she will smile, feeling content to believe
in the impossible.

Broke in West Berlin

I'm slouched in a phone booth off the Kurfürstendam, waiting
for a call that will never come.
I don't know why I live my life in short bursts,
burning like crazy until the money runs out,

then letting everything disappear in a puff of smoke.
I'm so down right now. I haven't really learned the way
this city works yet. At night everyone has to be happy;
crowds of elated Germans fill the streets.

How do they do it? They speak so fast,
even after years of education I still can't understand a word
of what they say. I do know, though, that
the German language is built for speed:

I can't imagine a German ever being broke, or if he was
he'd just invent a word for being penniless
and honorable, so he could hold his head up.
Where I come from, out of a job and money can only be warded off

by travel. If I were in America and broke
I'd hit the road, but now I can only wait
to hear from some girl who speaks Polish or something,
I don't know. This evening is wasted.

There's nothing for me to do, really,
except go back to the boarding house
and the angry looks of Frau Hauptmann
as I wander in at three in the morning. I wish I had,

or had had, one true love. An excuse for being
so maudlin. But the night will dwindle away
like hair through my fingers and I hope nobody minds
if I just fall asleep in this phone booth.

1988

Flowers

The woman behind the counter at the flower shop—
the one with the pince-nez and the British accent—
gives me a look like "What are you
doing in here, trying to send somebody flowers?"
Her suspicions are correct: I don't have enough money
for these Inca Marigolds, these Rosario Liles, these Achillea
Cerise Queens. I tell her I've forgotten my checkbook,
I'll be right back, but she knows I'm lying,
and she knows I know she knows I'm lying. It's no good.

But lately, I've been having flower dreams—
friends will be rising from the grave,
growling and drooling, and poppies
will burst from their empty eye sockets;
I'll be eating an ice cream cone
and it will turn into a rose; waking,
I expect a shower of daffodils
to fall from the ceiling and cover me.
I wanted to send you some flowers,
but that's not going to work out.

So I'll just have to send you my dream,
the one where you come to me, arms outstretched,
smiling, camellias opening in your palms.
You hold me close to you, and I can hear flowers growing,
and I wonder what I am doing here
in the midst of all this beauty.

Fragile

I awoke this morning to the sound of a bird
crying in the fireplace. It must have fallen
down there through the chimney, and now
it was trapped. I took the shivering form out
and held it to the light: small and greasy,
but not pitiful. . . . Is *fragile* the right word?
I fed it egg yolk through an eye-dropper and put it in a box.

Fragile is not the crystal goblet
packed in bubble-wrap and tissue paper. It is a deep,
soft-skinned thing; if it had a home it would dwell
in basements, its eyes shining in the dark
at anyone who comes down there. Fragile is this
young father who sits in the hospital waiting room
staring at his hands, after his daughter
has been grazed by a car: five years old, wandering out
to the middle of the road while he was gone
for five minutes, getting milk.
Now he feels like strips
of thin ice laced together. He feels invisible, he feels
that if he got up from the plastic chair he would plunge downward
for hundreds of miles.

The tiny bird that sat on my thumb had a look
in its eyes as if it were still falling down the chimney.
It must have been awful, that falling, the sooty darkness
of the fall. Who can go on living
after that? There is always the memory
of helplessness, always the possibility of balance reversing
itself: when gravity comes sucking up through a hole
sun-seared in the ground
to grasp hold.

En Route

The pool is full of salt water from the Adriatic.
It turns my skin to typing paper,
my hair to straw.

Two women sprawl in the shallow end of the pool;
the pale sun shines on their faces. Then one leans over
and kisses the other, her hand slinking

into her friend's bikini bottom. Is desire a cherry bomb
that goes off within them? I live
in a two-dimensional plane, all by myself, a geometric hermit,

watching two olive-skinned women make love
in a hotel pool in Rimini. . . .
But this is a memory: the strand of hair

left on your pillow, a note
written on the back of a receipt, sitting by your open window.
We are beginning our descent, the NO SMOKING light is on.

And so I have to get used to the airplane around me:
the executives reading *People* magazine, the lights
of Kansas City, Missouri, shining

like stolen jewels spilled at my feet.

Down the Coastal Highway

She's absolutely drunk.
She spent our last twenty dollars
on three bottles of wine
and a *Star* magazine: she drank the first
bottle and read the magazine while I was paying
for our room, she drank the second when we stopped
for breakfast at Joey's Beachside Pancakes,
and she's drinking the third now
as we speed down the coastal highway. She plays around
with the radio dial, the rap and country
stations drifting in and out of range,
puts her feet up on the dashboard and tells me
how lonely she is. When she was ten
she would ask her parents to
pick her up and hold her, just hold her
and they never would. She says
she hates it, cruising the beach towns
to buy beer for the high school kids,
anything to be with people, just sitting
holding hands with some pimply suburban geek
at his parents' condo. Then she starts crying,
she asks me if I'll hold her, right now.
I can't do that in the passing lane
so we pull over to the next rest stop,
and she crumples up in my arms
like there's no weight to her at all,
and she wants me to hold her tighter
so I do, until she stops crying and either
passes out or falls asleep
and I sit there listening to the ocean
rush up to meet the rocks.

The Names of Cities

I wanted to write a poem about a woman
who leaves her husband on a farm in Montana
to hitchhike for a week and reach
a city, where she takes up a room
and starts a new life. She'd
ride fourteen hours straight
in the passenger seat of an eighteen-wheeler
next to a trucker named Alan R.,
whose face would be covered with brushstrokes of stubble
the way jimmies are scattered all over
the chocolate doughnuts he'd eat from a box
as he drives. I guess the cheapest room
she'd be able to rent would be the one
right under the train tracks, and she
would have to learn to go to sleep
with the endless clatter of the El train
above her the way she learned to take the seasons
back home as they came: bathtubs full of hard snow,
generation-long dry spells, the sun
flexing its flames like a fist above her.
She would probably learn that this life
is no better than any other, that the sky
still turns to asphalt in the summer
and to linoleum in the winter, that city rain
makes her face ache with cold
the way tears never could, and that you can't
make an honest living shucking corn
or ironing shirts.
I don't know
exactly how my poem would end. Maybe with some
hysterical drama: murder or scandal,
a trail of blood, mumbled incantations;
or simply, with her marrying again, and joining
that throng of happiness we're promised is out there.

Maybe with her just leaving again
and hopping trains till she ran out
of places to go. What else is there to say
about her? For instance, what color
are her eyes, green or brown? Or does she
tie her hair back behind her
when it gets in her face? Even the city
she's come to, I don't know about that
either. This country is so full of cities
that I can't begin to tell about them
all. I could sit up and say
the names of cities all night
and into the morning, and the list would go on
and on, long after everyone in the cities
had fallen asleep.

Two

1977

The silver fish was packed in ice.
I looked at it through the smeared
window where it lay beside other fish.
How could it return my gaze?
It was dead, but its
huge round black pupil,
rimmed with crinkly silver
and glazed with clear matter, held me.

Holds me. Not the eye
of God but the fish's eye on me,
in me when I close
my eyes. Indifferent, unjudging,
but scary. (I was five.) What could have
an eye that big
and blank? Silent
universe in which our earth is just a speck.

Silence

We rest against the wall
in silence, sharing
an apple. I startle you
when I ask if you want the last bite.
Your eyes blank
to mine, your silence
is a garden, a comfortable
country of your own in which
I am a foreigner: I'm thinking
about silence, writing poems
in my head about silence—
there is a city inside
a darkened cave. When I light
a match to see the people,
the huts, the river winding
through silent streets the city
disappears.

Six years old
I sat on my mother's bed
as she brushed her hair, imagining
myself buried alive: I crouched
in a dark dusty chamber, shrieking
for rescue till my throat bled. Above,
the cemetery was silent, dry
leaves whirled around the headstones
as the sky turned from purple
to black—"What's wrong?"
she asked me, and I could not
speak.

You smile, biting
into the apple—the sound
is louder than the clank

of a thousand shovels, digging up
the children and the cities, digging
through fear and dirt
to what is buried underground.

Kathy's Dream

Rain, and the long
"row of objects." Kathy's teacher leads her
down the row, stopping at every one,
and commands her "to describe each of them
in less than ten seconds." Standing
before a skull she whispers

It's a monkey's face
It's a face you've seen before
It's the face in the window

—How can I
forget that face? Not the dead
one's, but my friend's: her own small skull and copper
hair wet in the rain. With her teacher's stern
eyes on her she scrunches her mouth, narrows
her gaze, looking at the slow-
crumbling bone clump, truly
seeing it, remembering
its name.

February

This is the third straight day of rain.
A homeless cat yawls somewhere by the woodshed—
the sound of something else's pain

at a remove is sometimes song-like. On the windowpane
and roof the drops are chunks of falling lead:
this third straight day of rain

and tearing wind has stripped me to my plain
wants: to be warm and dry, bundled up in bed,
where the sound of something else's pain

is far away. The cat moans on in a harsh refrain
out there by the soaked woodpile and busted sled,
while this third straight day of freezing rain

turns into night. Is there a mind that can contain
that sound without changing it to anything else instead
of the sound of something else's pain

without beginning or end—not try to explain
that creature's wail? Where are you: skinny, soaked, unfed
one lost out in the third straight day of rain?
The air's drenched with the sound of something else's pain.

Teenage Lust

I light a cigarette and menace passes through me,
as if the smoke that uncoils from my nostrils
could scatter disease and snuff out distant townships.

The driver of this car is going too fast. We are passing
through whole states in seconds.
Nobody can catch us. The girl upon whose shoulder

I rest loves me, and what's more—she'll stand up for me.
Don't mess with her. My cigarette crackles as I draw on it;
its dull-orange cherry thrums. Before I go to bed at night

I ask myself if I am happy with this life of smoke,
speed, and true love. The question pulls itself apart in my brain
as I sleep, and I wake with an answer coating my lips.

My Mother's Handwriting

After her mother died
I started saving every scrap of paper
With my mother's handwriting on it:
Little notes, postcards, random directions
Inside used matchbooks, dates scrawled
In afterthought on black-and-white snapshots.

I had seen my grandmother
Deep in sickness: tubes slinking out from under
The white gown, her skin yellow
And purple in patches, her thin mouth
Heaving past consciousness for the stale
Hospital air. At the mortuary

I saw my mother looking as if the breath
Had been pressed from her: she stood there staring—
Not sure how to move in a world without
Her mother in it? Right then I looked at her name
In the guest register: its steady schoolchild's cursive,
Strokes and loops I'd never really

Seen before. I could not imagine the one whose hand
Had held the pen wasted, and then laid out
Like that. I did not want to. I do not want to
Ever not see her before me, talking with, looking
At or away from me. I watch my futility
Pile to the ceiling: scribbled-on receipts and old address books

Rising around me, though they do not protect me. . . . Those inky
    curves
Will not replace her unbreathing body—even the opened
Envelope-flaps her living tongue has passed across.

Catalog of Tools

In the basement a scruffy, hulking refrigerator, loaded with six-packs,
 whose freezer was so frost-furred
Only a marble could have fit inside, droned away; each winter
 morning the boiler—its smooth, cylindrical surface
Too hot for fingertips—clanked and pinged itself awake, while the
 washing machine and dryer,
Just below the wooden stairs' dry rasp, made squishy, metallic
 tumbling sounds; and like a nearby gnat-throng,
Tubes of cold, sickly-green fluorescence buzzed almost
 imperceptibly. The poured concrete floor—
Scored with oval-shaped hollows and ridges like a wall-to-wall
 model of the moon, and painted mouse-fur gray—
Reflected watery daylight from windows set at ground level in shiny,
 slick-looking patches. Against one wall
A work-table and set of metal shelves brimmed with tools only my
 father's hands knew how to use: so ruddy
They were almost toast-colored, dense with hair, their pinkies' top
 joints larger than my thumbs, they sifted through
Heaps of all-sized screws and nails that overflowed from plastic
 trays, from kitchen-match boxes.
My hands—pale pink and soft, barely bigger than a doll's—fidgeted
 at my sides, stubbornly scared
Of the sandpaper, gritty as his unshaven cheek, that lay in a drawer
 alongside chalkstick-sized hunks of solid glue
I'd watch him feed into a small black gun whose trigger he depressed
 to heat the glue, then squirt it out
Like molten cheese from a beak-like metal tip (what a sinus-scraping
 smell!) onto a square patch of rubber
For his jogging shoes' broad soles. Drying afterwards, they sent up
 acrid waves of sweat from their perch
Atop the boiler (panting in the doorway each night, shorts stuck to
 his legs, he was so different from the man
Who'd left for work in suit and tie: his skin gleamed and reeked with
 a glaze so thick I shrank

From touching him—salty drops tipped each hair along his chest
and arms, drenching his mustache).
The hammer, its handle's rubber sheath spotted with holes, weighed
my hand down, but he hefted it
With ease, raising the blunt head brusquely up to *thwack* each nail
into the wood; the gangly saw *boinged*
When he flopped it back and forth, and made a kind of zipper-
crunch slicing through two-by-fours. A massive
Iron vise clenched the corner of his workbench, its lever rounded at
each end, corkscrew-striped, and cool
To my touch; I'd screw its lobster-red jaws tight, straining harder
with each turn, then slowly pull them apart
Along a slotted track that squeaked. How many hours did I sit there
looking up into his face
Shadowed in that sallow half-light, sweat inching down his brow as
mercury bubbled obscurely behind
The level's brittle glass and sportscasters called out plays I didn't
understand from a paint-flecked radio?
It seemed impossible that I would ever learn to hold the caulking
guns and bulbous-handled wrench,
Razor blades (each sleeved in thin cardboard), measuring rods, and
bright yellow nylon rope looped into arcane knots
As easily as he did, those long, unspeaking afternoons we spent
together halfway underground.

Late March

All day the sky
Gushes ice, and the neighborhood is glazed gray, silenced
Under frozen sleet. Against my window the drops reflect
No light or hue—the undercolor we return to after the spectrum
Has spent itself, gone out on a rage of burnished red,
Green, teeming yellow. Those are not
For us to keep. What is
Is gray, and a meaning
Of gray: blankness of black shading
To white, and back again. I did not want
To sit like this and see the sky
Cloud-smothered, the glass a shifting template
Of water, and beyond that the parking lot where an abandoned
    school bus fades
Into a memory of itself. Where the world was
Is nothing, which persists, and covers
Everything, and blazes
In its own way.

Days of 1995

Last night you stepped out from behind the wooden dream-door.
It's been so long, I've almost lost your face: now I find
you've waited in the back-office of my mind—
not even getting older, sleeping on the floor

or in the double bed we shared, half-empty
all this time. We were so unhappy. Our whispered
conversations in the pleading dark, all those words
I spoke to the back of your head—*Why did you? Why can't we?*—

must be somewhere in there, too; and the winter meals
we ate in sullen silence; dishes I could never get clean
enough; all the cigarettes I smoked in the kitchen,
afraid of your footsteps at the door. (My heart quickened, still,

at the key's rusty turn.) That day we stood and screamed
at each other outside the travel agency: I thought
I was right; I still do, even though I can't remember what we fought
about. Now that it doesn't matter, I wonder how it seemed

to you. Whatever became of the meager love
we made in that bedroom on the fourth floor—
or was it the third? From my side of the closed door
I can hear your muffled footsteps move.

Fossil

The dog limps off past the shoulder of the road;
Two women get out of the car to look for him.
Beside the highway a gravel yard stretches back, truckloads
Of small gray rocks piled high as sand dunes in the sun. Here also
Are abandoned tractor parts, engines and crank shafts rusting to soft
    brown, the spilling-out entrails of human machines—
As someday the bumper of the car that smashed the dog's side
    will rest
At the edge of scrub woods, next to the hacked-out stumps of trees,
    filling up with rainwater.

The women stand squinting into the sun.
Somewhere behind one of the gravel piles lies the dog, crumpled and
    bleeding, his cracked ribs jagged inside him.
Does he want to lie still, his blood coagulating in the dust, until he is
    a speck
Smaller than the component granules of these gray rocks? Flies
Wheel around him, patiently treading the matted stickiness of
    his skin.
Already his skeleton arches toward the sun, waiting to
    be cleansed
Of its flesh burden. Soon this fossil will be all that is left
Of the dog: alert skull and knobs of spine, high vault of the ribs
    where his heart was,
While pistons pump under the hoods of cars going past.

Kissing Alice

All week we've been waiting
to lean against the frosted-over window
of Buddy's Soda Shoppe, and make out
the whole afternoon: our hands
stuffed in each other's pockets as we suck
on each other's earlobes, the melting ice
around us an awkward angel
on the glass.

Then the other me
comes walking by, sees the two of us
kissing and kissing, wanting so much
to be one of us. . . . I am a snowman
standing here with a pipe in my mouth,
with my frozen carrot nose and coal eyes.
Will anyone ever want to touch me?

And the other Alice
perches on a naugahyde stool
inside Buddy's, letting her french fries get cold
as she watches us smudge the glass;
she drags her straw along the bottom
of her malted cup, slowly sucking
up the pink, icy dregs.

Before I Turned to Walk Away

I've been sitting alone all afternoon
in the library reference room, the day
of the morning when the look in my lover's eyes

said, *Don't come home.* Last week's newspapers
pile up on the table, I get up to wash my face
leaning over a water fountain, and remember

those men in the Port Authority bathroom—
one wrung his shirt out over the sink,
another lay down on grimy tile floor with a magazine

for his pillow. . . . How quickly
I washed my hands and rushed past
them, whose eyes followed me out, as if to say, *I know*

where you're going, their palms laid open
for the coins nestled, glowing, in my pocket.
I run my fingers over the day's stubble

on my face: when will I shave it off, and where?
In the mirror of the public bathroom
I see in my eyes the knowledge

those eyes burned
on the back of my mind
before I turned to walk away.

The Worms' Reply

> O worms! Black comrades without eye or ear,
> Here comes a dead man for you, willing and gay;
> Feasting philosophers, sons born of decay,
>
> Come burrow through my ruins, shed not a tear;
> But tell me if any torture is left to dread
> For this old soulless body, dead as the dead?
>
> —Baudelaire, "The Gladly Dead" (tr. Jackson Mathews)

Starving, we'll feast on your bloated paunch
for breakfast, leaving your thighs for lunch;
the wrinkled wineskin of your scrotum—still
half-full of that gray, tepid juice you people
use to make more of yourselves—we'll linger
over for dessert; your earlobes, too, and fatty fingers
are a snack for languid afternoons; and O the treat
of the spongy pads on your stilled feet
that once walked, arrogant, over the dirt,
our moist abode. Boring through your linen shirt
and poplin slacks, munching your socks full of holes,
we're glad you mislaid your meddling soul
in the sunlit world. "What's left?" you might ask: well,
although you cannot squint or touch or smell
you'll still possess acutest consciousness
of the way your paltry, flesh-bound usefulness
dwindles, as tenderly you're nullified.
Of course you'd hoped that, having died
once, you could repine and sulk at peace
eternally—but until, piece by piece,
we shit your gristle out (it takes so long!)
you're not finished. Dead man, you were conned
by hope of nothingness, heaven's negative:
toothless, we'll gobble all you still believe
as you recline under this mound
of dirt. Settle in for the stripping-down.

Dominion

A thin slab of slate is laid across
The tin bucket full of ashes. Along its edge
Moves a line of tent caterpillars, fuzzy
And stubborn, on their way somewhere. They lift
Their sectioned bodies
Out into the air, swaying there
Far above the dirt and grass—rows of undulating legs groping
For the next solid crossing. Not ten
Or twelve of them, but hundreds, probably
Thousands, writhe and twist on the slate, the grass, the steps
To this house, and lower themselves down from the trees around
    it: silent
And sightlessly persistent. Not in praise
Or emulation do I defer to them—this one
Climbing the crinkled silver rayon of my pants—but in
Defeat, my arms laid down, I watch them crawl
From the grass to the wall and up through the window into
    this poem.

Two Dreams

1.
You hold me close
to your chest, climbing up the hill.
You are huge: your heart
swells beneath my ear, your hands
cover my back. My hands
hold hard to your shoulders.
You are old: your skin
is grainy against my soft skin; I'm crying
into your white hair. You are older
than my father. You hold me
tighter than my father ever held me
climbing up that hill.

2.
Suddenly the newborn falls
right out of the sky
into my hands: transparent, fish-tiny,
barely breathing: and I have to watch it
die. It's over before I know: one
last rasp, then it congeals, curls up
in my palm, and I have to carry
it around the county fair with me
all day, holding it out
to everyone I meet, saying *Look*
look here is my child

Jane Cooper

for her seventieth birthday

Tonight I stand under the tree
outside the mottled glass
of your old office window. For weeks
I've watched its clenched buds
swell in the melting air—tonight it flares
with thousands of white blossoms. I feel like a child
down here, watching the brown knotted branches surge
skyward, entangled, embattled, lifted now
by each blossom-petal whose fragrance sheaths
and stills me.

Under the image
of flower, the hard work of flowering.
Winter of branches protected
only by ice, naked in the dull gray
light, is also an image. Something in the root-tips buried
under frozen ground was gathering,
wanting to live
as thick petal beneath April
sky—for how long before this night?

How long have I been
standing here, taking for granted
what was not meant to be but stubbornly
is, stretching above and around me, after
what struggle I only begin to know?
How can I stand here, child
of that struggle, and not give
thanks by asking *how?*

Three

Twenty-five

My teenage students write poems mourning themselves
at four and five: *I stood on a stack*
of milk crates, singing. . . .
Will I ever sing like that again?

I watch them, heads bent
over their notebooks, remembering
myself at fifteen, when poems
coursed down my arm to the page. If I could lift my pen
in the light of that long-gone attic window again. . . .

In New York my friend's face
is fine as vellum with her eighty years. Once
she sent me the French poet's words
in a letter: *You will weep for this hour in which you weep.*
It will go by too fast,
Too fast, like all the hours.

A Glimpse

One day I passed a numberless door
I'd never seen ajar. Larger than a closet, but not
Quite a room—it could have been a nun's praying-chamber;
Or some large cubby for dilapidated things: a cyrillic typewriter
Choked with sawdust; moth-gnawed bowler hats; or a place where
    the punished
Sat, alone. Approaching, I saw a mop with grimy
Jellyfish-tendrils dangling down; a plastic bucket—dungeon-gray,
On wheels—with a slotted well and handle to squeeze
The wet mop out; and a broom, its sweeping-part fringed
With mahogany bristles like a necklace of mustaches. A card
    table sat
Against the unwindowed wall, an open newspaper and radio,
    antenna up,
In mute still life on top. I'd only seen him once or twice,
The man who stoically (it seemed) sweeps and washes down
These halls, who must empty out the trash cans every night
(Though I'd never seen him doing that). My knee-jerk mind asked,
Is this where he sleeps? before clamming up. No figure
In a fairy tale, he goes home after work just like the rest
Of us. It was no glimpse into the afterlife,
Where the dead gather in bored and sullen packs;
No secret lovers heaved, giggling, on the linoleum; but all
I can remember of that afternoon is the sudden glance
As I hurried on my way—important papers in my hand?
Someone calling after me?—down a hall so clean
It squeaked under my feet.

Two Love Poems

We first kissed a year ago, in the concrete alley
behind my apartment: wooden steps connecting
floor to floor, tomato plants, that dried-up sponge,
an old collapsing table by the basement door:
above us the sooty emerald salt sky over Capp Street,
almost crowded out by telephone wires and the high,
weather-worn wall of the next building: back there
in the alley whose closed-in corners are home
to the skinny, matted, mistrustful,
raspy cats who fight and mate all night in the dark.

*

First I lodge my fingers
deep, deep at
the roots, then pull
them out
slowly, trailing along the thick,
wired length of your hair's
catalog of brown: darker
than this wooden table, close to black,
and lighter, too, a gold and cherry color streaming
into red when touched by light. I love
its electric tangle's resistance
to brush and fingers—each strand
vivid, distinct from the rest—together
they rise up from your head
in a swell of umber, red, and gold,
untamable.

Meditation at the County Landfill

All over fat gulls lunge
and swerve to forage in the mounds
of trash, their ruffled wings

and bellies cement gray,
their screeches mixed with dozers' scraping
groans and the garbage trucks'

harsh grind. The window down,
I breathe a burning mayonnaise smell
that scorches my nose and mouth:

a stink denser than air
and clogged with grit. This place looks
like a field where clumps of garbage

grow, these gloved men breathing through
dust masks its harvesters; "Park over here,"
one in sunglasses shouts

above the wind. I've come
to unload a rented house's junk—
at least ten years of things

that other people left
behind: a television, screen smashed
in to show its metal brain-stem wrapped

in multicolored wires; thick stacks
of mold-sheathed newspapers;
a roofless dollhouse. "Just dump it

there," barks a guy in overalls
when I ask what to do with all
this stuff. A quarter-mile away

there's a precipice: what for?
And then I see far off, a dozer
scooping up compacted

heaps and hurling them
below: so *this* is the place
debris is shoveled

underground to rot
until the end of time
(unless time's already

ended here). Barehanded,
I hurl these wet, grimed,
viscid chunks

of someone else's life onto
the reeking earth, startled
at the way this ruin

pleases me: as my sweat mixes
with the rising chalky
slime, I wade waist-high

through mounds that by
tomorrow will lie shoved
beneath a ground that has

no choice—it must accept
this offering. "Keep it coming,
man!" the masked face roars.

June 2, 2004

When you were scarcely out
of your mother's body the paperwork
began: a nurse hurriedly filled out forms
with her eye on the wall-clock,
her blood-smeared latex gloves
already in the trash can as you bawled
on the scale. So commonplace
(for her) that otherworldly newborn yowl.

Last Seen

Getting up at two o'clock to pee, I almost trip over our curled up,
exhausted dog, snore-shivering on the floor. Those four nights
he was gone, his asking face and dappled red-brown shape

wandered my sleep, while miles off he walked subdivision streets
in search of home. What did he eat—cat food left out in cans
for hardened strays, pizza box scraps, or nothing? The light

of six o'clock woke me from those dreams, but in the kitchen
I remembered the DECEASED ANIMAL dumpster at the pound:
who opens it each morning, and lifts with latex-covered hands

those sticky, still-warm shapes? The quiet, heaving sounds
were our mingled sobbing by the dish-stacked sink. You said
his name—*Griffin*—and those syllables set off another round

of sobs, our eyes red as the woman's who, shaking, held
up a snapshot to the pound's front desk guy. "Have you seen
this girl? She's been gone all afternoon." Shaking his head,

he looked away. She showed us all: brown hair and skin,
plastic barrettes, a ruffled blouse—"The school didn't call
me for five hours"—then ran back to her car. Standing in

the lobby, I held my flyer with his picture, *REWARD* scrawled
in marker underneath, and wrote his age and name,
the color of his eyes, then tacked it up with all

the rest: *LAST SEEN, PLEASE CALL*, each almost the same
as the next—so the streets we'd searched became one leaf-piled,
outspreading vacantness. That girl inside the frame

who'd leaned awkwardly against a fence and smiled
was somewhere in the infinite afternoon. From the car
her mother scanned every passing child's

face: some almost hers—then not all. How could I share
the least of what that woman knew? Her acrid smell
sputters, persistent, in my mind. . . . As Griffin makes sharp,

scared-sounding whines, I watch his body swell
with breath, and touch the places where prickly burrs
hugged his skin; footpads scraped to tender scabs, hungry and frail,

he can only sleep. How easily he vanished into a fissure
I hadn't known was there. I want to erase
those four days, but the images won't disappear

so fast: in the dark her tear-streaked grimace
surges forth; along the highway anonymous, mangled forms
lie waiting for a flashlight to illuminate each face.

Griffin's Coat

Griffin's coat is splotched
beige and dusty taupe on top;
underneath, these mingle
to a dried blood shade laced with strands
of gray, and silken-thick. My fingers
plunging through it seem
naked with their measly tufts
of blond knuckle-hair below
skin chill-pink and clammy
after rain. But where's
his skin? Raking my hands
in and out of this shaggy opulence
I can't find anything but fur,
which hourly frees itself from
him in wispy clumps and spreads around
the house until it's every-
where: Alyssa pulled one from her
eyelash last night, and when
he gets up from my lap
this sweater will be sheathed
in it. He doesn't care. He wants
my fingertips as deeply in
his coat as they can go, until
his amber eyeballs roll
backward under closed lids,
until my joints pulse
with the ache of holding him.

Beneath the Gingko

I lie all afternoon beneath the gingko, shadow-sheltered by its branches dense with skate-shaped leaves: their broad heads
And tail-like stems move with sea-creatures' languid swing in the wind. It's like being far below
The ocean's mottled skin, to sit under the reaching tree's branch-layers, as sunlight strains itself feebly
Down through them: eyelash-thin, dark emerald now, each leaf's every vein is clear to see,
And each vein casts a shadow-thread on every leaf's green-yellow skin. So many leaves!
In their shaggy density are jagged patches where the white-blue sky shows through—
Patches that reflect themselves in shimmer-spots along the ground, which send light up along the weeds' drooping,
Folded stems, the worn-out pair of walking shoes atop the concrete steps, and the steps
Themselves faded to raincloud-gray. Now the wind comes up again—the leaves make shallow *whooshes*
Like sea-waves far above; just as it frets the leaves it touches me, warm and liquid
On my neck and shoulders. Don't skim me any more than this, long wind: just to sit
With you and this familiar tree is almost all I ask; let me hear the freight train's song of rust
Low in your throat. . . . Wind among the leaves, leaves that hold the wind: soon
It will be too dark to sit outside.

Amsterdam Avenue

I rove ever back to a place
in my mind where your crotch is sweetly
pummeling mine.

Mission Street

Eyes at my feet, I prowled
sidewalks, parking lots,
scanned the gutters,
peered into flower pots,
my fingers itching
for discarded butts.

The best were firm, round,
barely smoked—furtively
I snatched each from the ground
and pressed it, still wet
from someone else's lips,
between my own;

but most lay crushed
into the sidewalk
and tasted of pavement, ash,
the soles of strangers' shoes,
barely distinguishable
from other bits of trash;

others pointed skyward,
lodged in viscous globs
of spit-out gum that clung to them
in taffy-strands as I drew
their filters out; some were tarred
with shoe- and tire-treads.

Scuttling ahead of me
amidst the prehistoric
smears—of what?—my gaze
ranged voraciously
into the dank interstices
of curb and street.

Wherever

Once, to be
someone, I had
to be some-
where—on the steps
of a cabin deep
in the woods, looking
up at the tin-foil sky;
or on a crowded
noonday New York
street, full of noise
and light, the press
of crowds. . . . I loved
those places and drank
in the coolness
of the trees and stars,
the heavy pulse
of chaos on the street.
But now
where I need
to be is beside
you, my hand lain
lightly in your lap,
your head wedged
up along
my shoulder, as we
look out at what-
ever is there—WALK
sign flashing its
green man, butterfly
resting on the iron
chair. Even to
sit without you (though
I miss you), knowing you
are sitting there,
wherever
you are, is enough.

For the Annapolis-Baltimore Railway Line

The bench under the waiting room window where the afternoon
    sunlight
Lay and the ticket counter's dusty glass top are gone, invisible
Within the new hotel's anonymous hallways. Behind the hotel a
    service road covers
The old train tracks, those lengths of steel and rotten ties
Pulled from the ground. As a child I walked along the tracks
Overgrown with wild grass, stretching
Down the length of West Street and out of town to Baltimore. I
    remember
How the grasstips scratched my face in the dwindling sun, as I
    looked out at the long line
Of telephone poles spilling their shadows
Into a field. Those afternoons with nothing to do—dawdling by the
    tracks
And in the woods, lying for hours on a patch of dirt
As clouds pulled by in nonsense shapes—are impossible
Now to hold as the actual shapes of those clouds, and the slant
Of sun on dirt. . . . On trains, sometimes, that sense
Returns, of being no one, watching through the smudged window
    the low roofs and chimneys of the slight
Midland townships: a rush of laundry
On the line, strips of grass, a woman's calico headscarf
And sloping shoulders, bright spinning pinwheel held by the child
Behind her—until I can become that woman
Up to her elbows in suds, or the child transfixed by the pinwheel's
    multicolored
Blur, the shirt pinned to the line, and the wind moving through each
Of its fibers. . . . And then it's gone, suddenly—far
Away from me as the city I've left behind, its streetlights just starting
    to come on
In the twilight. Gone is that child who lay beside the tracks,
    breathing
In the trees and light surrounding me, until they were a part

Of me. Gone that station, where the generations
Waited for trains from Richmond, Norfolk, Durham,
Chattanooga, watching for the chugging specks of those trains
    approaching,
Loaded with passengers, loaded with coal, coal shoved into
The furnace to become fire,
Smoke, ash.

Poem with Words by Jules Supervielle

"Beau monstre de la nuit . . ."

Beautiful monster of night, lay your purple cheek
on my window, shine out from starlight's cold stores.
After so harsh a silence, when will you speak?

Now that the daylight's grown thin and bleak
(and I'm dusky, too, deep in my rusted-out core)
beautiful monster of night, let me lay my cheek

on your shoulder. The dry branches creak,
and rocks hold their own on the forest's cold floor. . . .
After so harsh a silence, when will you speak

to me, protector? I've grown so worn and weak
that just to stand up's an impossible chore:
beautiful monster of night, lay your wizened cheek

on mine, raise me up—make me velvet and sleek,
walk me through twilight's oak door
after silence exhausts me. Then, will you speak

your name to me? O whisper, mumble, shriek
that sound I've spent my whole life waiting for,
beautiful monster, with your terrible, star-stubbled cheek
of silence, silence, silence. When will you speak?

945 Pecan Place

Since ten you've been standing behind a cash register, passing
vermicelli, skim milk, chicken breasts, and bottles
Of carbonated water over the scanner's secret red eye. "Will that be
ATM or credit? Would you like a bag?" Before noon
An embalmed-looking woman, her nails lacquered purple, held up
your line asking for "a *small* bag of cat litter—
You've only got the large ones." This Sunday afternoon squeaks by
on a conveyer belt, counted out in pennies and clammy nickels;
Wan sunlight across the asphalt and squashes' lichen green are the
colors you survive on while the clock's minute hand
Twitches, stuck, at 1:32. Back home, I gulp down toaster waffles and
lukewarm coffee, not even changing
Out of yesterday's socks, caught in a paperback Trollope's sticky
pages. Will Violet Effingham marry "comely" Phineas
Or the red-bristled reprobate, Lord Chiltern? I jerk the ring up to
my knuckle and back, the letters
Of our names stamped inside it collecting sweat and tiny bits of
skin. Our names are also printed on the checks
We wrote all yesterday afternoon: $68.74 to Pacific Bell, $45 to
Sutter Medical, etc.; now our bank account is empty
As Griffin's water dish. After I fill it up, he runs over to drink in one
long, barely-punctuated slurp, then ambles off,
Leaving a trail of drool-drops. On the day-long drive home from our
wedding, he lay crammed in the backseat
With the luggage, barely able to stretch his legs. By Ashland, bored
as he was, we started singing interstate ditties—
"There goes a gas station, here comes a cow"; after a while we
petered off into silence, Redding and Sacramento still
Hours ahead. The next day I squatted in the driveway to scrape a
thick layer of squashed bugs from the fender
With a toothbrush. Was it only four months ago? The vastness of
our lives—our life—pools about me till it seems
We have spent years in this run-down suburban house, our
paychecks never lasting long enough, too tired most nights

To do any more than hold each other in the dark, while Griffin
    wheezes plaintively. But love, common
As the oranges on our neighbors' tree, spreads half-unseen beneath,
    around us, even as you stand waiting
For the credit card authorization to pass along hundreds of miles of
    telephone line, your eyes fixed on the stacked
Shopping baskets, while I sit folding laundry in the bedroom,
    impatient for your worn-out footsteps at the door.

Notes

Daylight Savings
"Why on earth his memory . . .": from Natalia Ginzburg's *Famiglia,* as translated by Beryl Stockman.

Twenty-five
"You will weep . . .": from Naomi Replansky's translation of Guillaume Apollinaire's poem, "Àl la Santé."

Acknowledgements

Thanks to Rodger Moody at Silverfish Review Press and Barbara Hamby for their belief in this book.

Thanks to the editors of the following journals and anthologies in which many of these poems first appeared, some in slightly different versions: *American Literary Review, The American Poetry Review, Barnabe Mountain Review, Beyond the Valley of the Contemporary Poets 2004, Crazyhorse, Elixir, Gargoyle, InDigest, Lyric, Mark My Words: Five Emerging Poets, the minnesota review, Passages North, Poet Lore, Sonora Review, Southern Indiana Review,* and *The Southern Review.*

A number of these poems appeared in the chapbook *Beautiful Monster* (Swan Scythe Press, 2003).

I am deeply indebted to the late Jane Cooper for her friendship and her readings of these poems.

Special thanks to Naomi Replansky, fellow poet and dear friend.

Thanks to the following writers for their friendship and editorial acumen: Sarah Creider, Alejandro Escudé, John Fulton, Kathy Garlick, Karin Gottshall, Marit MacArthur, Jack Marshall, Sandra McPherson, Lisa Sperber, Sharan Strange, LB Thompson, and John Venable. Additional thanks to the many other friends, mentors, and editors who have worked with me on these poems.

Thanks to my family for their support and encouragement.

To my wife, Alyssa Sherwood—I love you.

The text and display types of this edition were set in Adobe Jenson, a faithful electronic version of the 1470 roman face of Nicolas Jenson. Jenson was a Frenchman employed as the mintmaster at Tours. Legend has it that he was sent to Mainz in 1458 by Charles VII to learn the new art of printing in the shop of Gutenberg, and import it to France. But he never returned, appearing in Venice in 1468; there his first roman types appeared, in his edition of Eusebius. He moved to Rome at the invitation of Pope Sixtus IV, where he died in 1480.

Type historian Daniel Berkeley Updike praises the Jenson Roman for "its readability, its mellowness of form, and the evenness of color in mass." Updike concludes, "Jenson's roman types have been the accepted models for roman letters ever since he made them, and, repeatedly copied in our own day, have never been equalled." The display types used for the cover are Helvetica Neue Bold Condensed and Black Condensed and Bodoni Antiqua Demi Italic. The cover text is set in ITC Bodoni Twelve.

Silverfish Review Press is committed to preserving ancient forests and natural resources. We elected to print *Best Western and Other Poems* on 30% post consumer recycled paper, processed chlorine free. As a result, for this printing, we have saved: 1 tree (40' tall and 6-8" diameter), 499 gallons of water, 293 kilowatt hours of electricity, 64 pounds of solid waste, and 120 pounds of greenhouse gases. Thomson-Shore, Inc. is a member of Green Press Initiative, a nonprofit program dedicated to supporting authors, publishers, and suppliers in their efforts to reduce their use of fiber obtained from endangered forests. For more information, visit www.greenpressinitiative.org.

Cover design by Valerie Brewster, Scribe Typography.
Text design by Rodger Moody and Connie Kudura, ProtoType Graphics.
Printed on acid-free papers and bound by Thomson-Shore, Inc.